ice lollies

AND OTHER FRUITY FROZEN TREATS

ice lollies

AND OTHER FRUITY FROZEN TREATS

RYLAND
PETERS
& SMALL

LONDON NEW YORK

Recipes by Sunil Vijayakar, Liz Franklin
and Elsa Petersen-Schepelern

Senior Designer Sonya Nathoo
Senior Commissioning Editor Julia Charles
Production Controller Toby Marshall
Art Director Leslie Harrington
Publishing Director Alison Starling

Indexer Hilary Bird

First published in 2011 by Ryland Peters & Small
20–21 Jockey's Fields, London WC1R 4BW
www.rylandpeters.com

10 9 8 7 6 5 4 3 2 1

Text © Liz Franklin, Sunil Vijayakar,
Ryland Peters & Small 2011
Design and photographs
© Ryland Peters & Small 2011

ISBN: 978-1-84975-106-3

A CIP record for this book is available from the
British Library.

Printed and bound in China

contents

the big chill

It is amazingly quick and easy to make your own delicious ice lollies and other frozen treats. Here you will find a collection of inspired recipes made with colourful combinations of fruits – from classic ice lollies (fruit purées, juices and sometimes yoghurt frozen solid in moulds), sorbets (simple flavoured sugar-syrup bases lightened with egg white), granitas (more granular than sorbets since the mixture is beaten not churned), sherbets (like sorbets but with yoghurt or fromage frais added), water ices (similar to sorbets but denser and more intensely flavoured) and frappés (flavoured fruit and sugar mixtures frozen and then blitzed in the food processor to make them smooth but thick).

All you need to make the recipes in this book are a good selection of conventional plastic lolly moulds with sticks, some novelty silicone moulds and a freezer compartment large enough to accommodate your chosen moulds. Innovative ice lolly makers are now available that freeze lollies in super-quick time so do look out for these – especially useful if you are making lollies for impatient kids! Ice cream makers can be used for making the sorbets – although they aren't strictly necessary, they do make the job faster and easier, and the texture slightly smoother. Happy freezing!

ice lollies

classic oj lollies

Commercially produced ice lollies are often packed full of sugar and unhealthy additives. Give your children these home-made ones and reduce the family's dental bills!

600 ml freshly squeezed orange juice

6 ice lolly moulds with sticks

makes 6

Pour the orange juice into the ice lolly moulds. Insert the sticks in the centre of each lolly and freeze for 4–6 hours, until completely solid.

When ready to serve, dip the moulds in hot water for a few seconds to loosen the ice lollies and serve immediately.

raspberry lollies

Delight in these ruby-coloured treats. For a fun stripy effect, alternate the raspberry mixture with orange juice, freezing each layer before adding the next.

750 g fresh or frozen raspberries

4 tablespoons runny honey

6 ice lolly moulds with sticks

makes 6

Purée the raspberries in the bowl of a food processor or in a blender.

Strain through a sieve to remove the seeds, then stir in the honey. Pour the mixture into the lolly moulds, insert the sticks in the centre of each lolly and freeze for 4–6 hours, until completely solid.

When ready to serve, dip the moulds in hot water for a few seconds to loosen the ice lollies and serve immediately.

peach and plum lollies

600 g fresh peaches
or nectarines

sugar or runny honey,
to taste

600 g fresh plums

6–8 ice lolly moulds with sticks

makes 6–8

This is a wonderful way to capture the essence of summer with the flavours and vibrant colours of ripe, juicy peaches and plums.

To make a peach purée, skin, stone and chop the peaches and put the flesh in a large saucepan with 200 ml cold water and sugar or honey to taste.

Bring to the boil, reduce the heat to low and simmer gently for 4–5 minutes. Remove from the heat and process until smooth in the bowl of a food processor. Taste and add a little more sugar or honey if necessary (this will depend on the ripeness of the fruit you are using).

To make a plum purée, follow the same method as for peaches but using unskinned, halved and stoned plums.

Carefully spoon a little of the peach purée into the base of the ice lolly moulds and top with a little of the plum mixture. Continue layering until the moulds are full. Insert a stick in the centre of each lolly and freeze for 4–6 hours, until frozen solid.

When ready to serve, dip the moulds in hot water for a few seconds to loosen the ice lollies and serve immediately.

mango, strawberry and passion-fruit lollies

400 g fresh mango pieces*
(or 500 ml prepared mango
purée if available)

12 large, ripe strawberries,
hulled and halved

4 ripe passion fruit

sugar, to taste

6–8 ice lolly moulds with sticks

makes 6–8

These icy treats are full of refreshing tropical flavours.
Part-freeze them between each addition to keep the
layers separate.

Put the mango pieces in a blender and whizz until puréed. Add
the strawberries and blend until smooth, adding a little water if
necessary, to achieve the consistency of thin cream.

Scoop the passion fruit flesh and seeds into a bowl and break
up the flesh up with a fork. Add sugar to taste, and stir until it
has dissolved.

Spoon a layer of the mango and strawberry mixture into each
ice lolly mould, filling them about one-third full. Transfer to the
freezer for about 30 minutes, until part-frozen. Remove from the
freezer and top up with passion fruit. Return to the freezer for
a further 30 minutes. (Do not allow the lollies to freeze solid or it
will be difficult to insert the sticks.) Insert a stick in the centre of
each lolly and freeze for a final 4–5 hours, until completely solid.

When ready to serve, dip the moulds in hot water for a few
seconds to loosen the ice lollies and serve immediately.

*Note: To make really good mango purée, buy the freshest,
ripest and sweetest mangoes available.

600 ml unsweetened pure cranberry juice

200 ml freshly squeezed orange juice

200 g caster sugar

10 small freezerproof moulds (such as silicone mini cupcake moulds or foil petit four cases) and 10 wooden ice lolly sticks

Makes about 10

cranberry and orange lollies

Cranberry and orange juices make a fabulous fruity combination, as any devotee of the Sea Breeze cocktail will attest. Simply delicious!

Pour the cranberry and orange juices into a bowl. Add the sugar and stir until it has completely dissolved.

Put the moulds in one layer in a suitable freezerproof container. Pour the mixture into the moulds. Transfer to the freezer for about 30 minutes, until part-frozen. Remove from the freezer, insert a stick in the centre of each lolly and freeze for a further 4–6 hours, until completely solid.

When ready to serve, dip the moulds in hot water for a few seconds to loosen the ice lollies and serve immediately.

yellow grapefruit lollies

about 6 yellow or pink grapefruits
(about 600 ml juice)

200 g caster sugar

an electric citrus juicer (optional)

6–8 ice lolly moulds with sticks

makes about 6

These delicious, thirst-quenching ice lollies are popular
with all ages, and all that vitamin C has to be a bonus.
Try this made with pink or ruby red grapefruit juice too.

Cut the grapefruits in half. Extract the juice using an electric
citrus juicer or a traditional juicer. You will need about 600 ml
of juice.

Pour the grapefruit juice into a bowl. Add the sugar and 200 ml
cold water and stir until the sugar has completely dissolved.

Pour the mixture into the moulds. Transfer to the freezer for
about 30 minutes, until part-frozen. Remove from the freezer,
insert a stick in the centre of each lolly and freeze for a further
4–6 hours, until completely solid.

When ready to serve, dip the moulds in hot water for a few
seconds to loosen the ice lollies and serve immediately.

tangerine and plum sorbet on a stick

800 g ripe plums

75 g golden caster sugar

2 sweet tangerines

1 small egg white

an electric citrus juicer (optional)

an ice cream maker (optional)

6 ice lolly moulds with sticks

makes 6

Almost any firm-textured, fruit-based sorbet can be frozen into a lolly (or any other ice moulds) to make a terrific healthy treat. Here, plum and tangerine are combined with delicious results.

Halve, stone and slice the plums. Put the plum flesh in a saucepan and add the sugar and 200 ml cold water. Bring to the boil then cover, reduce the heat to low and cook for 4–5 minutes, or until the sugar has dissolved and the plums are just tender.

Transfer the mixture to the bowl of a food processor or a blender. Cut the tangerines in half. Extract the juice using an electric citrus juicer or a traditional juicer. You will need about 100 ml of juice. Add the tangerine juice to the food processor and blend with the plums until smooth. Allow the mixture to cool.

When cool, transfer the mixture to an ice cream maker and churn until thick. If making the sorbet by hand, place the mixture in a shallow freezerproof container and freeze for 4 hours until slushy.

Whisk the egg white in a grease-free bowl until frothy and add to the mixture in the ice cream maker. Continue to churn until thick enough to scoop. If making by hand, simply mix the egg white into the slushy mixture with a fork, whisk, electric hand mixer or spatula to break up the ice crystals. Spoon the mixture into the ice lolly moulds. Insert a stick in the centre of each lolly and freeze for 4–6 hours, until completely solid.

When ready to serve, dip the moulds in hot water for a few seconds to loosen the ice lollies and serve immediately.

fruit gelato lollies

500 g each of ripe peaches, plums, apricots or other soft fruits of your choice (except kiwi fruit, as they will curdle the milk)

300 g sugar

For the gelato base:

1 litre whipping or single cream

5 very fresh egg yolks

250 g caster sugar

18 ice lolly moulds with sticks

makes 18 (6 of each flavour)

These creamy lollies are made with a classic Italian 'gelato' ice cream base. The recipe produces a large quantity so divide the basic mixture into three 500-ml portions, and add a different puréed fruit flavouring to each one.

To make the gelato base, pour the cream into a saucepan and heat gently. Beat the egg yolks and sugar together in a bowl until pale and creamy. Beat 2 tablespoons of the hot cream into the egg mixture, then beat in the remaining cream, little by little. Pour into a heatproof bowl set over a pan of simmering water, and cook over gentle heat, stirring constantly, until the mixture coats the back of a spoon. Set aside to cool.

Put the peaches in a saucepan with 100 g of the sugar and sufficient water to cover. Bring to the boil, then simmer until cooked but not too soft. Remove from the pan and slip off the skins, cut in half and remove the stones. Transfer to the bowl of a food processor. Boil the cooking liquid until reduced to about 250 ml, then let cool. Purée the peaches in the food processor, adding enough cooking liquid to make 500 ml. Chill. Repeat with the plums and then the apricots (or other fruit of your choice).

Divide the cooled gelato base into 3 batches and add a different fruit purée to each portion. Spoon the mixtures into the ice lolly moulds. Insert a stick in the centre of each lolly and freeze for 4–6 hours, until completely solid.

When ready to serve, dip the moulds in hot water for a few seconds to loosen the ice lollies and serve immediately.

maple and peach frozen yoghurt squares

250 g fresh ripe peaches

500 ml natural yoghurt

125 ml pure maple syrup

an ice cream maker (optional)

6 freezerproof moulds (about 5 cm square) and 6 lolly sticks

makes 6

Here yoghurt is flavoured with maple syrup and peaches to create a deliciously indulgent yet healthy lolly. You can vary the flavour of the yoghurt and use different fruit to create your own favourite recipes; pineapple works well.

Peel and stone the peaches and finely chop the flesh. Put the yoghurt in a large bowl and stir in the maple syrup. Fold in the chopped peaches and mix until well combined.

Transfer the mixture to an ice cream maker and churn according to the manufacturer's instructions, until firm enough to scoop. If making by hand, pour the mixture into a shallow freezerproof container and freeze for 2 hours, whisking the partially frozen ice at least once with a fork, whisk, handheld electric mixer or spatula to break up the ice crystals.

Spoon the semi-frozen mixture into the moulds. Insert a stick in the centre of each lolly and freeze for 3–4 hours, until completely solid.

When ready to serve, dip the moulds in hot water for a few seconds to loosen the ice lollies and serve immediately.

mint julep sticks

300 g caster sugar

50 g fresh mint leaves,
finely chopped

15 ml Bourbon (optional)

mint leaves, to decorate

*6 small freezerproof moulds
(such as silicone mini cupcake
moulds or foil petit four cases)
and 6 ice lolly sticks*

makes 6

This is a grown-up icy treat, perfect as a fun apéritif or perhaps a light dessert on a balmy summer's evening. To make a child-friendly version, simply omit the Bourbon.

Put the sugar in a saucepan with 600 ml cold water. Heat, stirring constantly, until the sugar has completely dissolved. Bring to the boil for 1–2 minutes, then take off the heat and stir in the chopped mint leaves. Set aside to cool completely.

When the mixture is cold, strain out the mint and add the bourbon. Pour into the moulds and push whole mint leaves into each one. Insert a stick in the centre of each lolly and freeze for 3–4 hours, until completely solid.

When ready to serve, dip the moulds in hot water for a few seconds to loosen the ice lollies and serve immediately.

crushed ice sticks

These delightful iced treats are enjoyed
in India (where they are known as 'golas')
and are the perfect way to cool down on
a hot summer's day.

300 g ice cubes

any fruit- or flower-based syrup or
cordial such as strawberry, lemon,
orange, blackcurrant, elderflower
or rose

6 wooden or bamboo skewers

6 small shot or liqueur glasses

makes 6

First, crush the ice cubes. Most blenders can crush
ice. If you have a food processor and not a blender,
it may not be possible to crush ice in it; check the
manufacturer's instructions. Alternatively you can
put the ice cubes in a strong polythene bag and
crush them by hitting them with a rolling pin.

Take about 50 g of the crushed ice in the palm
of your hand and mould it around the end of a
wooden or bamboo skewer, squeezing tightly so
the ice forms into a rough ice lolly shape.

Pour the syrup of your choice into the glasses, to
come up halfway. To enjoy, dip the 'gola' into the
syrup and then suck the syrup through the ice.

frozen treats

cranberry and mango bars

250 g fresh mango pieces*
(or 300 ml prepared mango
purée if available)

300 ml unsweetened pure
cranberry juice

*6 freezerproof rectangular moulds
(the plastic liner tray from a box of
cake slices or biscuits works well)*

makes 6

Sharp cranberry juice and sweet mango make for an interestingly sour-sweet flavour combination. This recipe couldn't be simpler and the bars look beautiful too.

Put the mango pieces in a blender and whizz until puréed, adding a little water if necessary, to achieve the consistency of thin cream.

Half-fill each mould with the cranberry juice. Transfer to the freezer for about 30 minutes (on a tray if your mould is a little flimsy), until part-frozen.

Remove from the freezer and top with a layer of the mango purée. Return to the freezer for a further 4–5 hours, until completely solid.

When ready to serve, dip the mould in hot water for a few seconds to loosen the ice bars and serve immediately.

*Note: To make really good mango purée, buy the freshest, ripest and sweetest mangoes available.

iced strawberry hearts

450 g fresh strawberries

50–75 g caster sugar, to taste
(this will depend on the sweetness
of your strawberries)

250 ml vanilla-flavoured yoghurt

*6 individual heart-shaped silicone
moulds or a baking tin with
6 heart-shaped holes*

makes 6

The classic combination of strawberries and cream is
a guaranteed favourite with everyone, but this heart-
healthy version is made with vanilla-flavoured yoghurt.
Show someone you care with this delicious frozen treat.

Hull and roughly chop the strawberries. Put them in the bowl
of a food processor or a blender and add the sugar. Process until
blended and smooth.

Half fill each mould with the strawberry purée. Transfer to the
freezer for about 30 minutes, until part-frozen.

Remove from the freezer and carefully add a layer of the vanilla
yoghurt. Return to the freezer for a further 3–4 hours, until
completely solid.

When ready to serve, dip the moulds in hot water for a few
seconds to loosen the iced hearts and serve immediately.

mini honey kiwi tartlets

4 ripe kiwi fruit

3–5 tablespoons runny honey, to taste

a drop of green food colouring (optional)

6 small freezerproof moulds (such as silicone mini cupcake moulds or foil petit four cases) and 6 ice lolly sticks

makes 6

The dull exterior of this fruit belies its pretty flesh so here is a great way to show it off and a fun way to enjoy their delicious flavour. For even more visual impact, you can add a couple of drops of green food colouring.

Peel the kiwi fruit and chop the flesh into chunks. Put in the bowl of a food processor or a blender and, adding the honey a little at a time, blend and taste – depending on the sweetness of the kiwis you may not need to use all of it.

Pour the mixture into the moulds and carefully transfer to the freezer. Freeze for 4–6 hours, until completely solid.

When ready to serve, dip the moulds in hot water for a few seconds to loosen the frozen tartlets and serve immediately.

mixed berry and citrus cones

500 g fresh or frozen mixed summer berries such as strawberries, raspberries, blackberries and blueberries

100 g icing sugar

200 ml freshly squeezed orange juice

1 tablespoon freshly squeezed lime juice

1 tablespoon freshly squeezed lemon juice

greaseproof paper

scissors

stapler

2–3 tall glass tumblers, or similar

makes 6

These dramatic-looking cones are bursting at the seams with fruity goodness, which makes them an utterly delicious and super-stylish way to get your five-a-day!

Start by making the moulds. Cut out six 15 x 30-cm lengths of greaseproof paper. Roll the greaseproof paper to form a cone shape, making sure that there is no hole at the pointed end, and staple to secure.

Put the berries in the bowl of a food processor or a blender and add the icing sugar. Blitz until puréed and smooth. Set a sieve over a bowl and pour the berry mixture into it. Use a spatula or large spoon to force it through the sieve and strain out the seeds. Put the orange juice in a small jug with the lime and lemon juices.

Stand the cone moulds upright in the glass tumblers to support them. Spoon in a layer of the berry mixture then top up with the citrus juice mixture.

Carefully transfer to the freezer and freeze, standing upright, for 4–6 hours, until completely solid.

To serve, invert the cones onto a plate and gently peel off the greaseproof paper.

marbled strawberry and blackberry yoghurt cups

250 g fresh blackberries

250 g fresh strawberries

8 tablespoons runny honey

500 g natural yoghurt

6 freezerproof cup-shaped moulds, each about 7 cm in diameter

makes 6

Colourful, tasty and healthy, these iced treats make a great 'snack-attack' standby. Keep a batch of these in the freezer for unexpected young visitors.

Put the blackberries in the bowl of a food processor or a blender and purée until smooth. Set a sieve over a bowl and pour the blackberry mixture into it. Use a spatula or large spoon to force it through the sieve and strain out the seeds. Set aside.

Hull the strawberries, put them in the bowl of a food processor or a blender and purée until smooth. Set a sieve over a separate bowl and pour the strawberry mixture into it. Use a spatula or large spoon to force it through the sieve and strain out the seeds. Set aside.

Add 2 tablespoons of the honey to each bowl and stir to mix well. Put the yoghurt in a separate bowl, add the remaining honey and mix well.

Spoon some of the blackberry mixture into the base of a mould. Carefully spoon over some yoghurt and then some of the strawberry mixture. Use a skewer or similar to lightly marble the mixtures together. Fill the remaining moulds in the same way.

Carefully transfer to the freezer and freeze for 4–6 hours, until completely solid. When ready to serve, dip the moulds in hot water for a few seconds to loosen and serve immediately.

fruity ice cube treats

sparkling mineral water or
soda water, to top up the trays

Choose from:

fruit slices

star fruit (carambolas)

unwaxed lemons

unwaxed oranges

kiwi fruit, peeled

black or white grapes

summer berries

blackberries

raspberries

small strawberries, hulled

blueberries

redcurrants, blackcurrants
and whitecurrants

green herbs

small basil leaves

small mint leaves

rosemary sprigs

lemon balm leaves

*silicone or plastic ice cube trays
(as many as required)*

Make these pretty fruit-filled decorations for summer drinks
and cocktails or add them to a large punch-bowl to create
a centrepiece for a garden party or barbecue. Experiment
with flavour combinations.

Prepare your chosen fruits or herbs, cutting them into pieces
to fit the size of the holes in your ice cube trays or leaving them
whole, as necessary.

Drop a whole fruit, slice of fruit or herb leaf into each hole.
Pouring slowly (ideally from a jug) top up each one with still or
sparkling water. Carefully transfer to the freezer and freeze for
4–6 hours, until completely solid.

Variation: You can also freeze pure fruit juices in the ice cube
trays and then add them to tall glasses of chilled soda water
or sparkling mineral water for a refreshing and eye-catching drink.

fruit ice blocks with buttermilk froth

a selection of pure fruit juices:
berry and tropical juices work well

100 ml buttermilk
or low-fat natural yoghurt

sparkling mineral water or
soda water, to top up

*1–2 silicone or plastic ice cube
trays, sufficient to make 16 cubes*

4 tall glasses or tumblers

serves 4

Freeze a selection of pure fruit juices in ice cube trays and serve them in a tall glass of frothy buttermilk for a delicious low-fat and nutritious treat on a hot day.

Pour the fruit juices into the ice cube trays and carefully transfer to the freezer. Freeze for 4–6 hours, until completely solid.

Add 4 fruity ice cubes to each glass. Add a dollop of buttermilk or yoghurt, then top up with sparkling mineral water or soda water. Serve immediately.

The ice cubes melt slowly into the drink, so you can top it up with more buttermilk or more mineral water for a long, cool, delicious and surprisingly filling drink.

pomegranate granita

This once hard-to-find fruit, a native of the Middle East, has a thick waxy skin enclosing hundreds of jewel-like ruby seeds. The juice is hailed as a great antioxidant and is now widely available in many shops.

600 ml pure pomegranate juice

200 g caster sugar

pomegranate seeds,
to decorate (optional)

serves 4–6

Pour the juice into a large, shallow freezerproof container. Add the sugar and stir into the juice until dissolved.

Cover with a lid and transfer to the freezer. Freeze for 2 hours, until the mixture starts to look mushy.

Remove the granita from the freezer and using a fork, break up the ice crystals and mash them. Return the granita to the freezer for a further 2 hours, mashing every 30 minutes, until the ice forms fine crystals.

After the final mashing, return to the freezer for at least 1 hour before serving. Decorate with the fresh pomegranate seeds, if using.

orange and lemon granita

Zing zing zing! Your taste buds won't know what's hit them. Zesty doesn't even begin to describe this wide-awake, citrus assault.

115 g caster sugar

6 oranges

2 lemons

an electric citrus juice (optional)

serves 4–6

Put the sugar and 200 ml cold water in a large saucepan. Using a vegetable peeler, pare thin strips of zest from 1 orange and 1 lemon and add them to the sugar and water. Heat gently, stirring until the sugar has dissolved. Bring to the boil and then take off the heat and let cool. When cold, strain through a sieve into a large, shallow freezerproof container.

Extract the juice from all of the fruit using an electric citrus juicer or a traditional juicer. You will need about 500 ml of juice. Pour the juice into the cool syrup and stir to combine. Cover with a lid, transfer to the freezer and freeze for 2 hours.

Remove the granita from the freezer and using a fork, break up the ice crystals and mash them. Return the granita to the freezer for a further 2 hours, mashing every 30 minutes, until the ice forms fine crystals. After the final mashing, return to the freezer for at least 1 hour before serving.

granitas and water ice

pink grapefruit and basil frappé

Frappés fall somewhere between granitas and slushes and can be eaten with a spoon or enjoyed through a thick straw. Refreshing and not too sweet, this grown-up recipe is flecked with basil and flavoured with its subtle aniseed tones.

220 g caster sugar

4 large pink grapefruit

50 g fresh basil leaves, finely shredded

an electric citrus juicer (optional)

serves 4–6

Put the sugar in a large saucepan and add 300 ml cold water. Add the zest of 1 grapefruit. Heat gently, stirring until the sugar has dissolved then simmer for 5 minutes. Remove from the heat and leave to cool.

Extract the juice from all of the grapefruit using an electric citrus juicer or a traditional juicer. You will need about 500 ml of juice. Strain the cooled syrup through a sieve into a large, shallow freezerproof container and add the juice and the basil. Stir well.

Cover with a lid, transfer to the freezer and freeze for 3 hours, until firm. Just before serving, transfer to a blender and crush until smooth.

rhubarb and ginger frappé

The ginger and rhubarb weave magic together in this bittersweet, spicy frappé, which is sure to delight all lovers of rhubarb.

750 g rhubarb, chopped

100 g caster sugar

a 2-cm piece of fresh ginger, peeled and finely grated

serves 4–6

Put the rhubarb, sugar and ginger in a large saucepan and add 100 ml cold water. Cover and cook over medium heat for 4–5 minutes. Remove from the heat and leave to cool.

Once cold, transfer to the bowl of a food processor or a blender and purée until smooth. Pour into a large, shallow freezerproof container.

Cover with a lid, transfer to the freezer and freeze for 3 hours, until firm. Just before serving, transfer to a blender and crush until smooth.

star anise and mandarin orange granita

150 g caster sugar

6 whole star anise

20 mandarin oranges

serves 4–6

Star anise and mandarin oranges are natural partners, as both originate in China. The star anise not only adds a wonderful liquorice flavour, it also looks stunning and makes for a very stylish decoration.

Put the sugar in a large saucepan and add 200 ml cold water. Heat gently, stirring until the sugar has completely dissolved. Add the star anise and simmer without stirring for 2 minutes. Remove from the heat and leave to cool.

Cut a slice off the top and bottom of each mandarin, then slice away the peel and pith. Chop the flesh roughly and put in the bowl of a food processor. Process until almost smooth. Press the resulting pulp through a sieve into a large, shallow freezerproof container. Strain the cooled syrup into the container, reserving the star anise, and mix well. Cover with a lid, transfer to the freezer and freeze for 2 hours, until the mixture starts to look mushy.

Remove the granita from the freezer and using a fork, break up the ice crystals and mash them. Return the granita to the freezer for a further 2 hours, mashing every 30 minutes, until the ice forms fine crystals.

After the final mashing, return to the freezer for at least 1 hour before serving. Decorate with the reserved star anise, if using.

watermelon granita

150 g caster sugar

1.75 kg watermelon

finely grated zest and freshly squeezed juice of 1 lime

serves 4–6

On a hot and sticky summer's day there is nothing better than sinking your teeth into a slice of refrigerator-cold watermelon. Nothing, that is, except this vivid granita with a tangy hint of lime.

Put the sugar in a large saucepan and add 150 ml cold water. Slowly bring to the boil, stirring until the sugar has completely dissolved. Once boiled, remove from the heat and leave to cool.

Scoop out the flesh from the watermelon and discard the seeds. Blitz briefly in the bowl of a food processor or a blender, until smooth. Strain the resulting pulp through a sieve into a large, shallow freezerproof container. Add the syrup, lime zest and juice to the same container and mix well.

Cover with a lid, transfer to the freezer and freeze for 2 hours, until the mixture starts to look mushy.

Remove the granita from the freezer and using a fork, break up the ice crystals and mash them. Return the granita to the freezer for a further 2 hours, mashing every 30 minutes, until the ice forms fine crystals.

After the final mashing, return to the freezer for at least 1 hour before serving.

blood orange water ice

8 large blood oranges

115 g caster sugar

an electric citrus juicer (optional)

an ice cream maker

serves 4–6

Blood oranges have been cultivated in Sicily since ancient times. An unassuming peel, tinged with purple, conceals a flesh ranging from rose in colour to almost black: pure drama, especially in this grown-up water ice.

Wash the oranges in hot water to remove any waxy coating.

Put the sugar in a large saucepan and add 200 ml cold water. Using a vegetable peeler, pare thin strips of the zest from 1 of the oranges and add to the sugar and water. Heat gently, stirring until the sugar has completely dissolved. Bring to the boil and then remove from the heat and leave to cool. Once cool, strain through a sieve set over a large bowl and discard the zest.

Extract the juice from the oranges using an electric citrus juicer or a traditional juicer. You will need about 600 ml of juice. Pour the juice into the strained syrup and mix to combine.

Pour the liquid into an ice cream maker and churn according to the manufacturer's instructions, until it just holds its shape.

Spoon the semi-frozen mixture into a large shallow, freezerproof container, cover with a lid and transfer to the freezer. Freeze for 3 hours. Remove from the freezer, beat for 1–2 minutes and return to the freezer for about 2 hours, until firm enough to serve in scoops.

sorbets
and sherbets

nectarine and almond sorbet

700 g ripe nectarines

75 g golden caster sugar

a few drops of almond extract

1 egg white

an ice cream maker (optional)

serves 4–6

This fruity sorbet is bursting with the flavours of a Mediterranean summer – ripe nectarines delicately flavoured with a hint of almonds.

Peel, halve and stone the nectarines. Thinly slice the flesh and put in a saucepan. Add the sugar and 300 ml cold water. Bring to the boil, reduce the heat to low, cover with a lid and simmer for 6–8 minutes, until the nectarines are just tender. Transfer to the bowl of a food processor or a blender and process until smooth. Leave to cool and then transfer to a bowl and chill in the refrigerator.

When chilled, add the almond extract and pour the mixture into an ice cream maker. Churn according to the manufacturer's instructions, until thick. Alternatively, transfer to a large, shallow freezerproof container, cover with a lid and freeze for 4 hours, until slushy.

Whisk the egg white in a grease-free bowl, until just frothy. Add to the mixture in the ice cream maker and continue to churn until firm enough to scoop. If making by hand, transfer the mixture to the bowl of a food processor and whizz until softened. Add the egg white, mix well and return the mixture to the container. Freeze for 4–6 hours, until firm enough to serve in scoops.

kiwi and stem ginger sorbet

115 g golden caster sugar

8 ripe kiwi fruit

1 egg white, lightly beaten

2 tablespoons stem ginger, drained and finely chopped

an ice cream maker (optional)

serves 4–6

This pale green sorbet is made using ripe kiwi fruit and is given a lively aromatic flavour with the addition of stem ginger. For a stronger flavour, omit the stem ginger and use a teaspoon of freshly grated ginger instead.

Put the sugar and 300 ml cold water in a small saucepan and heat gently until the sugar has completely dissolved. Bring to the boil and remove from the heat. Leave to cool and then transfer to a bowl and chill in the refrigerator.

Peel and roughly chop the kiwi fruit. Put the flesh in a blender and process until smooth. Add the resulting pulp to the chilled syrup and mix well.

Pour the mixture into an ice cream maker and churn according to the manufacturer's instructions, until thick. Add the egg white and stem ginger to the mixture and churn until firm enough to scoop.

If making the sorbet by hand, pour the mixture into a large, shallow freezerproof container and stir in the egg white. Cover with a lid, transfer to the freezer and freeze for 3–4 hours. Scoop into the bowl of a food processor and whizz until smooth. Return to the container, stir in the stem ginger and return to the freezer for a further 3–4 hours, until firm enough to serve in scoops.

chilli-lime sorbet

A twist on the classic lemon sorbet, this refreshingly tangy sorbet has a hidden kick.

200 g golden caster sugar

1 red chilli, deseeded and very finely chopped

6 large limes

1 egg white

an ice cream maker (optional)

serves 4–6

Put the sugar and chilli in a saucepan and add 300 ml cold water. Heat gently until the sugar has completely dissolved. Bring to the boil, remove from the heat and finely grate the zest of 2 of the limes directly into the mixture. Leave to cool, transfer to a bowl and chill in the refrigerator.

Extract the juice from all of the limes using a juicer and add to the chilled syrup. Pour the mixture into an ice cream maker and churn according to the manufacturer's instructions, until thick. If making by hand, freeze the mixture in a freezerproof container for 4 hours, until mushy.

Whisk the egg white until just frothy. Add to the mixture in the ice cream maker and continue to churn, until firm enough to scoop. If making by hand, whizz the semi-frozen mixture in a food processor, add the whisked egg white and return it to the container. Cover with a lid, transfer to the freezer and freeze for 3–4 hours, until firm.

blueberry sorbet

This deliciously sharp sorbet is bursting with the wonderful flavours of summer.

500 g blueberries

150 g golden caster sugar

finely grated zest and freshly squeezed juice of 1 lemon

1 egg white

an ice cream maker (optional)

serves 4–6

Put the blueberries and 150 ml cold water in a saucepan and bring to the boil. Remove from the heat, let cool and process to a purée in a blender.

Put the sugar, lemon zest and juice and 200 ml cold water in a saucepan and heat gently, until the sugar has completely dissolved. Bring to the boil then take off the heat. Let cool, transfer to a bowl and chill in the refrigerator.

Mix the blueberry purée with the chilled syrup. Pour the mixture into an ice cream maker and churn according to the manufacturer's instructions, until thick. If making by hand, freeze the mixture in a freezerproof container for 4 hours, until slushy.

Whisk the egg white until just frothy. Add to the mixture in the ice cream maker and continue to churn, until firm enough to scoop. If making by hand, whizz the semi-frozen mixture in a food processor, add the whisked egg white and return it to the container. Cover with a lid, transfer to the freezer and freeze for 3–4 hours, until firm.

apricot and grape sherbet

100 g caster sugar

12 ripe apricots

150 ml pure unsweetened white grape juice

300 g low-fat natural yoghurt or fromage frais

an ice cream maker

serves 4–6

A perfectly ripe apricot is a rare and wonderful treat, however you enjoy it and this sherbet is no exception. An ice cream maker is essential here for a smooth result.

Put the sugar in a large saucepan and add 150 ml cold water. Heat gently until the sugar has completely dissolved. Halve and stone the apricots and add to the pan. Simmer for 5 minutes. Remove from the heat and leave to cool.

Put the apricots and cooled syrup in the bowl of a food processor or a blender and process until smooth. Press through a sieve set over a large bowl. Discard any pulp left in the sieve and stir the grape juice and yoghurt into the apricot mixture.

Transfer the mixture to an ice cream maker and churn according to the manufacturer's instructions, until firm enough to serve in scoops.

spicy plum sherbet

This cold-yet-warming sherbet is perfect for those late summer days when plums still abound yet there is a decided nip in the air.

120 g caster sugar

1 cinnamon stick

4 cloves

a 2.5-cm piece of fresh ginger, peeled and thinly liced

12 ripe plums, halved and stoned

375 g low-fat natural yoghurt

an ice cream maker

serves 4–6

Put the sugar, cinnamon, cloves and ginger in a large saucepan and add 100 ml cold water. Heat gently, stirring until the sugar has dissolved completely. Halve and stone the plums and add to the pan. Simmer for 5 minutes. Remove from the heat and leave to cool.

Once cool, discard the cinnamon and cloves and transfer the plums and syrup a blender. Process to a purée. Press through a sieve set over a bowl and stir in the yoghurt.

Transfer the mixture to an ice cream maker and churn according to the manufacturer's instructions until firm enough to serve in scoops.

raspberry sherbet

Pink, creamy and luscious – this sherbet sounds far naughtier than it actually is! Fresh berries and fat-free fromage frais make for a delightfully low-fat treat.

120 g caster sugar

375 g raspberries

375 g fat-free fromage frais

an ice cream maker

serves 4–6

Put the sugar in a large saucepan and add 100 ml cold water. Heat gently, stirring until the sugar has dissolved completely. Bring to the boil then remove from the heat.

Put the raspberries in a blender and process to a purée. Press through a sieve set over a bowl and discard the seeds. Stir the cooled syrup into the strained raspberry purée. Transfer the bowl to the refrigerator and chill well. Add the fromage frais to the purée and whisk until smooth.

Transfer the mixture to an ice cream maker and churn according to the manufacturer's instructions, until firm enough to serve in scoops.

index

recipe credits

Sunil Vijayakar

Apricot and grape sherbet
Blood orange water ice
Blueberry sorbet
Classic OJ lollies
Chilli-lime sorbet
Cranberry and mango bars
Crushed ice sticks
Fruity ice cube treats
Iced strawberry hearts
Kiwi and stem ginger sorbet
Maple peach frozen yoghurt squares
Marbled strawberry and blackberry frozen
    yoghurt cups
Mini honey kiwi tartlets
Mint julep sticks
Mixed berry and citrus cones
Nectarine and almond sorbet
Orange and lemon granita
Peach and plum lollies
Pink grapefruit and basil frappé
Pomegranate granita
Raspberry lollies
Raspberry sherbet
Rhubarb and ginger frappé
Spicy plum sherbet
Star anise and mandarin granita
Tangerine and plum sorbet on a stick
Watermelon granita

Elsa Petersen-Schepelern

Fruit ice cubes with buttermilk froth
Fruit gelato lollies
Mango, strawberry and passion fruit lollies

Liz Franklin

Cranberry and orange lollies
Yellow grapefruit lollies

photography credits

All photographs by **Richard Jung** unless otherwise stated below

William Lingwood
Pages 14–15, 16, 41

James Merrell
Page 20

Debi Treloar
Page 12